MY
DARLING
HUSBAND

WHO IS A HUSBAND?

THE
CORNERSTONE
PUBLISHING

E. O FARINTO-OLURINTO

MY DARLING HUSBAND
Copyright © 2020 by **E.O Farinto-Olurinto**

ISBN: 978-1-944652-96-8

Published By:
Cornerstone Publishing
A division of Cornerstone Creativity Group LLC
Info@thecornerstonepublishers.com
www.thecornerstonepublishers.com

Author's Information
For speaking engagement or to order bulk copies of this books please call +1 929-436-8673

To the Blessed Holy Trinity - God the Father, the Son and the Holy Spirit - by whose help, many exploits have been accomplished in my Christian journey.

ACKNOWLEDGMENTS

My profound appreciation goes to the Almighty God, who gave me the inspiration to write this book. I also appreciate the contributions of all the vessels of honor that God has been using to support me and my ministry at THY WILL BE DONE INT'L GOSPEL MINISTRIES.

Very special thanks to my wife, Lady Evangelist Esther O. Farinto, for her dedication and support to the ministry.

With a grateful heart, I say "thank you" to my spiritual mentors and role models, Evangelist Oguniran, Pastor Samuel Gbadebo, Prophet/Reverend Gbeleyi, Pastor (Very Rev.) Professor C.M.A. Ademoroti and Pastor (Mrs.) Agbeja (U.S.A.), for their progressive impacts.

I also appreciate my son at Datamasta Computer Ltd, Ilesa Branch, who carefully typeset the manuscript of this book. May God bless you all.

CONTENTS

INTRODUCTION

I want to congratulate every sister, who, by divine arrangement, gets to read a copy of this book. You must indeed be special in God's sight. From the time of inspiring the writing of this book, the Holy Spirit has told me that it would only get into the hands of a selected number of ladies. I therefore congratulate you again for being one of these chosen ones. This book is one of my contributions to fostering harmony and resolving conflicts in the home.

Satan did all he could to hinder this work, so that you would not be able to come across the powerful revelations about marriage that it contains. Through it all, however, the Lord has greatly magnified Himself. I assure you, sister, this book will tremendously transform your marriage and life in general. Even if you are yet to be married, know that you are about to have an unforgettable experience that the Holy Spirit has prepared for your home. Moreover, the Holy Spirit warned me that having a copy of this book is not as secure as reading, digesting and applying its messages.

You are about to attain such level of victory that will

see God leveling every mountain, filling every valley and straightening every crooked path in your marital journey. To bring this to fulfillment, let us begin by asking the following foundational questions:

1. Why do you want to marry?
2. What brought you to this conclusion?
3. Who told you he is your God-ordained husband?
4. Did you confirm it spiritually?
5. If you are married already, who is your husband to you? For instance, Sarah's husband (Abraham) was lord to her (1 Peter 3:6).
6. What is the purpose of your being married to the man you are with?
7. Did your biological and spiritual parents consent to your marriage with him?
8. What is likely to be the end of the family you are raising on earth?

As you will soon find out in the course of reading this book, it is necessary for you to ponder the above questions. The answers which many other ladies faithfully provided to these questions paved way for their marital happiness. My prayer is that God will make you escape the shame, reproach, dishonor, disgrace and disregard that come from separation, divorce, widowhood, or inability to get married to the right man.

Please note that every message in this book is a direct

revelation from God on choosing the right husband and living with him. Whatever the Holy Spirit reveals is always in tandem with the Bible. I therefore counsel that you read this book along with your Bible. This will also help you to crosscheck the messages here before accepting or rejecting them. Be like the Berean Christians (Acts 17:10-11).

There are many women who could have made great achievements in life but became handicapped because of one crisis or the other in the process of choosing, marrying and living with a man. If you are yet to marry, therefore, I particularly thank God for your life. As you discover the pitfalls in the marital journey as discussed in this book, the Holy Spirit will enable you to make spiritual adjustments from stage to stage. Revelation, inspiration and renewal will definitely flow into your life, in Jesus name.

CHAPTER 1

YOUR FOUNDATION MATTERS

"If the foundations be destroyed, what can the righteous do?" (Psalm 11:3)

Foundation is a timeless and universal phenomenon. Everything on earth, from the beginning of time, has a foundation – or what you might call a starting point. The earth's physical structures, the cities, the homes, the businesses, the organizations and the governments do not hang in space. They all have a foundation. In fact, the earth itself has a foundation. Zechariah 12:1 says, "The burden of the word of the LORD for Israel, saith the LORD, which stretcheth forth the heavens, and layeth the foundation of the earth, and formeth the spirit of man within him."

In a similar vein, God's throne is described as having the foundation of righteousness and justice (Psalm 97:2). Abraham is considered the father (or foundation) of those who demonstrate absolute faith in God. The children of Jacob founded the twelve tribes of Israel. The Apostles pioneered the Early Church, while the foundation of the spiritual Church is Christ Himself. Most importantly, the Lord Himself is the foundation of Christendom and the salvation of souls. Believing and receiving Him as your personal Savior and Lord establishes your faith in God.

PERSONAL AND MARITAL ANGLE

Just like the heavens and the earth, as well as everything else we have discussed so far, everyone in the world has a "foundation". So also is every marital union. Now, a person's foundation could be good or bad, weak or strong, godly or demonic, pure or polluted. One thing is certain, however: Your foundation determines whether you will live a life of freedom or of bondage. Moreover, just as the foundation of a building determines how high it can go, so also does the foundation of a person affect how far he or she can go in life. This is why the issue of foundation must be taken very seriously

Foundations are the fundamental structures upon which lives are built. The marital foundation, in particular, is vitally important to the success of our sojourn on earth. Since foundation determines ultimate destination, it becomes pertinent for every woman to keep eternity in view at every stage of life, so as to achieve a glorious building. Pay good attention to this because only God's special mercy and supernatural intervention can help to mend a faulty foundation – especially one that has to do with marriage!

MAKING GOD YOUR FOCUS

It is of great importance that you allow God to be your guide and guard as you embark on the marital journey. Let Him be the Lord, every step of the way, so that you will not stumble (Proverbs 3:5-6).

Apparently, God was the foundation of the relationship between Adam and Eve. However, because they were not totally focused on God, Satan came in and distracted them from God's presence and purpose. Nevertheless, the Scripture affirms God as the architect of Adam's life and marriage (Genesis 2:7, 18-24). He therefore remains the one and only perfect match-maker, who you must rely on at all times.

Genesis 24:1 reveals to us that God's hand of favor was mightily upon Jacob, despite all the troubles he passed through. The reason was because he acknowledged God in all his dealings. Indeed, concerning his destiny, God's pronouncement was "…Jacob I have loved; But Esau I have hated" (Malachi 1:2-3). Unsurprisingly, while Jacob's life overflowed with God's blessings, Esau's life was full of miseries - because He did not involve God in his affairs.

We find a glaring example of Esau's willful determination to manage his own affairs in his decision to marry women from an ungodly lineage. Despite the severe grief that his decision brought upon his parents, he was not remorseful in any way. Prior to that, he had despised his birthright for a morsel of pottage. Eventually, he missed the blessing that should have been conferred on him and his generation (Genesis 27). His generation thus became irrelevant since he had long received a curse that he would serve his younger brother, Jacob.

This is the foundational truth I am emphasizing here. Every individual has powerful truths hidden in his or her roots. We need to find out what these truths are and change every changeable before they ruin our lives and relationships. Similarly, any man to which you are married will form a strong pillar of your children's foundation and will ultimately influence your life and future for good or for evil.

Most importantly, however, the best foundation you can lay is to have a solid relationship with Jesus Christ. You must surrender your all to Jesus because without Him and His help, you cannot amount to much in life, let alone making a success of your marital journey (see John 15:3-5). Ensure that the foundation of your marriage is Christ, the Rock. This way, the covenant blessing will be yours for eternity.

EXAMINING YOUR FOUNDATION

As you begin to think of getting married as an eligible

lady, you need to understand that you are on the verge of laying a foundation for an upcoming generation. You have so much to put into the groundwork for a successful accomplishment.

You and your intended husband can unconsciously make an indelible mark on the sand of time that will affect the destinies of your unborn children. This is why I cannot stop emphasizing the need for you to thoroughly seek the face of God to help you not to make a wrong choice. You must ever be on your guard against the devil's devices, just as you continue to bear in mind that he has his own evil agenda against every marriage plan.

One sure way that the devil always seeks to execute his destructive program in anyone's life is to mislead them into marrying the wrong person. When this is achieved, the devil easily manipulates the marriage and progressively diverts or destroys their destiny. Such faulty marital foundations have derailed many women from God's will. For such women to recover their destinies, as well as those of their offspring, they need deliverance through anointed ministers of God.

Once again, foundations are of very great importance. Look at the family of Lot and what became of his children and their descendants. It all began with Lot laying the wrong foundation of choosing to raise a family in the land of Sodom, which, together with Gomorrah and the surrounding cities, was notorious for sexual perversion (Jude 1:7). Things were so bad that, as early as those times, homosexuality had become very common in the city. This wrong foundation affected the thinking and behavior of his daughters, such that when they each needed a man to be intimate with and none was immediately available, it never occurred to them to consult God to make a way for them. Instead, they got their aged father drunk with wine and made him sleep with them in turns. This resulted in the two sisters having children through their father - an abomination of the highest degree (Genesis 19:30-38).

With this ungodly act, the daughters themselves ended up laying a foundation of cursing for their children and those who would come after them. It was through their children that the accursed nations of Moab and Ammon came into existence. In a nutshell, the faulty foundations laid by Lot on the one hand, and the one later laid by his daughters ended up negatively affecting the generations of children that came after them.

There is a lot to learn from the missteps of Lot and his daughters. And I will say his daughters especially because this is a book for women and the decisions taken by Lot's daughters in their moment of desperation went on to affect their innocent offspring. To make this study more practical, therefore, I will request you to find a way to politely ask your mother a few but definite questions about your foundation. I refer to your mother, because mothers often have more accurate knowledge about a child's conception more than anyone else.

Without any bias in your mind, prayerfully and tactfully ask your mother the following questions:

- How did you meet and married my father?
- Did someone play a middleman role for my father? If yes, who?
- Did you sleep with my father before you two were married?
- What was the religion of my father and yours as at the time of the wedding?
- Did you visit a spiritual home to conceive me?
- Are you really sure my father is my father?
- Did you take my pregnancy to any native doctor or spiritualist?
- Did anything significant or unusual happen the day I was born?
- Who took my delivery?
- Who took my placenta and where was it buried?
- Was I a welcomed or a rejected child?
- Did anything significant or strange happen during my naming ceremony?
- What kind of naming ceremony was done for me? Was it a Christian, Islamic or traditional type?
- Did you have any serious quarrel with anyone

around the time of my pregnancy or birth?

These are some of the vital questions you need to ask your mother and they are direct pointers to your foundation. Each answer provides a clue to your existence and deliverance. So, once again, make sure you prayerfully approach your mother on this mission.

FOOD FOR THOUGHT

Friendship is the root of relationship, while relationship is the mother of courtship and courtship is the foundation of marriage. Obedience and total submission are the flavors of LOVE, but interest and care are its paternal and material grandparents. Please, watch whom you want to join your life with as your future partner, and follow the process as directed by God and His word. It is then your future will not be regrettable. Jesus says it clearly, "Therefore whoever hears these sayings of Mine, and does them, I will liken him to a wise man who built his house on the rock: and the rain descended, the floods came, and the winds blew and beat on that house; and it did not fall, for it was founded on the rock.

"But everyone who hears these sayings of Mine, and does not do them, will be like a foolish man who built his house on the sand: and the rain descended, the floods came, and the winds blew and beat on that house; and it fell. And great was its fall" (Matthew 7:24-27).

CHAPTER 2

THE EIGHT DIFFERENT TYPES OF MEN

"Most men will proclaim every one his own goodness: but a faithful man who can find?" (Proverbs 20:6)

Men in general can be categorized into seven distinct groups, according to their potential marital behaviors. They are:

THE "GOOD" MAN

The good man is always a socially appealing and acceptable individual. Unfortunately, he misuses his acceptability to amass various types of women for himself. This man may have money and good family background. He is naturally handsome, wears good clothes, and is always neat. He may even be very smart and wise like Solomon. Yet, this does not automatically make him a potentially befitting husband for you. For instance, with all the blessings and wisdom of Solomon, he wasn't seriously committed to any of his wives – despite the fact that he was a good man! The Bible reveals that He was always in love with worldly women (1Kings 11:1). No wonder his name was excluded in the genealogy of Jesus Christ (Luke 3:23-38).

THE CONCUBINE

A concubine is a man who is only interested in having sex with a woman or using her in any other way to meet his social, career or financial needs.   A concubine can destroy a home totally. If, for instance, he enjoys a woman more than her husband, he could go to the extent of killing the husband. I have seen a man who loved his wife very much, but later, his wife fell in love with another man. When the husband knew about the affair, he asked his wife but she denied it. He then started to watch her movement. When the wife told the concubine about her husband's   questions, the concubine found a way to severely harm the man. This is just one case among several.

A concubine is not a husband; in a few years, he will take another woman as wife and when you ask him about it, he will tell you not to worry - that she is just a friend; until he marries up to seven women and they eventually chase you out of your home.

THE STRANGE MAN

This is a man who, though marries a wife wholeheartedly, does not care for her. He is more interested in making money by any means. – including sacrificing the welfare and even the very lives of his wife and children. It is men who belong to this category that get involved in cult and familiar spirit initiations. Many of them are possessed and their children are all over town, looking for whom to marry. This is why ladies must have an idea of the kind of parents any man proposing marriage to them has before giving their consent.

Strange parents have been in the game of manipulation and destruction for longer than you can ever know. Their children are in higher institutions and workplaces everywhere, and many of them are very influential. If care is not taken, if you marry any of their strange sons, it means you have entered into a cursed family; even a child you give birth to may be used for money rituals in the   future.

Some years back, I met a boy in serious sickness. He had been medically diagnosed and treated many times but there was no cure to his sickness. It was at this stage that I was called to pray for him. As I prayed, the Holy Spirit spoke to me that he had been long pegged to take over his father's position in occultism, but he had refused. The cult group had therefore vowed to deal with him.

Such occult men are scattered all over. They are the foundation of many of the evils on earth; they pollute streets, towns and even countries. Anywhere you go, you will meet them there, posing as if they are godly, but it's all a lie.

THE WIDOWER

This is a kind of man who has got spiritual a problem that ensures that whoever he marries must die prematurely. He has been covenanted with evil spirits that he will not have a wife or that if he has a wife then she must die young. In western Nigeria, there are some places where if you get married to their daughter as a non-indigene, their idol will attack and kill you. In some other areas, if their daughter gets married to a non-indigene, it is a problem. There are parents who, for whatever reason, hate their son's wife. There are even those who don't want their sons to marry at all. They love to take care of their sons themselves than allow him to get married. Whoever marries these types of men is risking her life.

THE HAPPY-GO-LUCKY MAN

This man is really and genuinely married and he loves to be identified with his wife and children. However, he is poor mentally, spiritually and financially. Worse still, he lacks ambition and has an excessively relaxed attitude towards life. Rather than engage in serious work, he prefers to indulge in gambling, betting, drinking, and loafing about. He is so financially wretched, yet believes that his life will soon change for the better. Naturally, this kind of man plays no   serious financial role at home. The wife takes care of the children and even his own feeding, while he celebrates with his friends from one relaxation spot to another! When he eventually returns home, he reels out a list of complaints and fictitious problems that are preventing him from discharging his normal responsibilities at home. No wonder the Bible says "Who hath woe? who hath sorrow? who hath contentions? who hath babbling? who hath wounds without cause? who hath redness of eyes? They that tarry long at the wine; they that go to seek mixed wine" (Proverbs 23:29-30).

Ironically, it is this kind of men that many ladies want to fall in love with. They easily entice ladies with their neat appearance, polite discussions, loud boasting about their achievements, and a long list of their engagements with highly-placed people. The careless, covetous lady never tries to doubt their integrity until she has given birth to two or three children and found the man's boastings to be totally void. It is then she will realize that she has married the wrong man.

Happy-go-lucky men are those who love to have children but have no time or resources to nurture them. They just know that they are married and have children. If anything happens to their in-laws, they are not ready to take any responsibility. This is the kind of man that ends up being called "useless". I pray you will not be joined to such in Jesus' name.

THE PROSTITUTE

There are lots of men who are prostitutes. They have their own wives, but are always searching for other women with whom they will commit adultery. The spirit of adultery dominates their entire being (Hosea 5:4), and they have a way of charming careless women to do their bidding.

THE ANGRY MAN

The angry man always batters his wife! He is married with children, but his demands from his wife are often so high and non-negotiable – so much that he hardly gives room for dialogue. He foolishly assumes that anger and violence are the key to resolving issues and having his way. This is why God strictly warns, "Make no friendship with an angry man; and with a furious man thou shalt not go" (Proverbs 22:24).

The angry man is often puffed up and feels highly proud of his competencies and achievements. Truly, he seems committed to the home, but his opinions and rules are final in all things. He has no regard for even his parents in his brutal dealings with his wife and children. Even his in-laws cannot talk to him. Whoever gets married to such a man because of his wealth will surely regret it.

All of the above mentioned men are everywhere. They continue to trouble ladies with their cruelty, lies and empty promises. They promise to perform in six months what they do not have the ability to do it in six years. Sister, believe me, none of these seven kinds of men is suitable for marriage. But don't lose hope...there is another kind of man!

THE IDEAL MAN

This is a true husband. A true husband is generally in love with his wife. Whatever her condition may be, he cares for her in sincerity. The ideal man will readily support you to achieve your dreams and aspirations in life. He is not out to hinder your destiny or to cover your star or glory. He is in love with your family. He does not seek to forcefully impose his will over you in any area of the family affairs. He always demonstrates compassion for each family member. He is ready for dialogue, and always   listens to your advice. He does not make use of worldly advice and wrong conversations to rule his home. He always feels your absence. He is not someone that will leave his family and go to a club and come back late in the night.

The ideal man does not mingle with bad company but with godly people. He is concerned about his children and asks about their progress in school and church. He always finds time to play with his children in the house; he does not discriminate among them. Nobody can condemn his wife before him and will receive his support because he believes that she is his best counselor and mother of the whole house. He is a discreet, focused and foresighted person.

No matter the situation, the ideal man keeps company with men of God. He attends church regularly and punctually, and participates actively in the things of God. He is very accommodating and always loyal to his wife in everything. He is also ever ready to take correction.

The ideal man always prays for the well-being of his family, including his wife's family. He also sends gifts to them as finances permit. He is always ready to assist his wife in any area. He does not relate loosely with the opposite sex, whether at home or at work. He maintains his integrity everywhere.

The ideal man is indeed a special gift to a woman from God. This is why you cannot locate him by your own wisdom; you can only locate him by total surrender of your will to God, with fasting and prayer, and with proper guidance and counsel from God's word.

CHAPTER 3

KEYS TO MARRYING THE IDEAL MAN

"Every good gift and every perfect gift is from above, and cometh down from the Father of lights, with whom is no variableness, neither shadow of turning." (James 1:17)

Having taken care of the foundation on which you want to build your marital life, the next step is to commence the building proper. This begins with knowing who your God-ordained husband is, out of the multitudes of men you will come across in life. Note again that regardless of how smart, knowledgeable or discerning you are, this is not something you can do on your own; you need God's leading and wisdom. But you will need to cooperate with Him by taking note of the following:

1. Avoid searching in the wrong places.

This is the beginning of failure for many women in marriage – getting married to someone from a wrong place. "Wrong place" here could mean wrong religion, wrong sources, or wrong kingdom. Wrong religion refers to any religion outside of Christendom; wrong sources include so-called professional match-makers and media advertisements; while wrong kingdom means "outside of God's Kingdom" – that is, someone not born again.

This means that someone may even be a member or a worker in a church and still not be suitable for you to marry, if he is not born again. No matter how nice, gentle or caring a person may appear to be, as long as he has no clear testimony of being born again, he doesn't belong to God's Kingdom.

The Lord strictly warns, "Be ye not unequally yoked together with unbelievers: for what fellowship hath righteousness with unrighteousness? and what communion hath light with darkness?" (2 Corinthians 6:14).

Therefore, you must never get so desperate as to marry someone outside of Christ or someone who has no clear evidence of genuine salvation, with the belief that you will "convert" the person. There is no one who has the power to convert a soul. Even in the work of soul-winning, ours is just to preach; only the Spirit of God causes conviction and conversion. Therefore, you cannot gamble over such a critical matter. This is why Paul expressly asked, "For what knowest thou, O wife, whether thou shalt save thy husband? or how knowest thou, O man, whether thou shalt save thy wife?" (1 Corinthians 7:16). He asked such a question because salvation is not what anyone can guarantee another person. It is strictly a personal matter.

Rather than taking any unwise step out of desperation, I encourage you to wait upon the Lord for His appointed time for you. God still speaks to His children today as He did in the past. He can speak to you through your dream, vision or through spirit-led persons. In fact, the message of God's word can sanctify your mind such that pure thoughts of revelation can be your possession. This is the way to be sure that God is fully involved in every step of your marital journey.

A true child of God will never search for a husband the worldly way or get so desperate for a man that she begins to manipulate men like the daughters of Lot (Genesis 19:31-32). Of course, I am aware that certain unpleasant situations such as joblessness, poverty, family pressure and bodily needs could tempt a lady to give in to advances from a successful unbeliever or a mere church-goer, but the real source of solution, as the Psalmist says, is: "I will lift up mine eyes unto the hills, from whence cometh my help. My help cometh from the Lord, which made heaven and earth" (Psalm 121:1).

The attitude of the Psalmist here is very instructive. He was determined not to look up to the world to meet his needs, but to the Almighty God – the only One Who knows the end from the beginning.

What I have realized from my years of counseling is that many women do not know that as females, they are designed to be a helper to a certain man. (Genesis 2:18; 1 Corinthians 11:8-9). In fact, Jesus categorically said, "Have ye not read, that he which made them at the beginning made them male and female…?" (Matthew 19:4). This means that there is a man for every woman and vice versa. It is certain therefore that with more prayer and patience, the right man will appear. Yet, many of these Christian women complain and murmur before God that they have waited too long. Some even go ahead to marry just any man. It is when they begin to see the true character of the man that they begin to realize that it is indeed good to wait upon the Lord.

Do you know the reason why Esau's generation became irrelevant in the Bible? It was because he married outside of his lineage! What about Lot? We have noted a few things about him and his daughters already. But the Holy Spirit actually made me realize that the primary reason he and his generation were plagued was because he married a Sodomite woman whose attitudes manifested in the lives of her daughters, as we saw earlier.

What all these reveal is that the family, community, culture or kingdom from which you marry will affect your future home and life. I believe Abraham was well aware of this – which was why he made his servant swear that he would never get a Canaanite woman for Isaac to marry (Genesis 24:1-4). On the negative side,

Samson went into the world to marry and he suffered the consequences (Judges 16:1). Mahlon and Chilion, the only two children of Elimelech and Naomi, also got married to Moabite women and they died untimely (Ruth 1:1-5). Some Israelites got into relationships with Moabite women and the anger of the Lord was kindled against them (Numbers 25:1-3). So, sister, avoid searching in the wrong places, so you don't get into an accursed marriage.

2. Locate and stick to your spiritual parents.

Once you have the determination to stay in the Lord, your spiritual parents will be encouraged to support your spiritual journey by way of counseling and moral support. These spiritual parents could be your natural parents who are mature believers themselves, or they could be trusted and spiritually-sound leaders in the church.

We have a good example of how spiritual parents function in Genesis 27:46, which says, "And Rebekah said to Isaac, I am weary of my life because of the daughters of Heth: if Jacob take a wife of the daughters of Heth, such as these which are of the daughters of the land, what good shall my life do me?" Heth is a tribe in Canaan, and the Scripture records that immediately after these words of concern from Rebecca, Isaac called Jacob and blessed him and told him, "You shall not take a wife from the daughters of Canaan. Arise, go to Padan Aram, to the house of Bethuel your mother's father; and take yourself a wife from there of the daughters of Laban your mother's brother" (Genesis 28:1-2).

It is a pity that many who should be spiritual fathers and mothers to young men in church today are themselves becoming abusive and falling into adultery. Still, the roles spiritual parents are of tremendous importance to every life. I particularly counsel you to listen to your father-in-the-Lord or your biological father, if he is in the Lord. Several Christian ladies start their marital plans by ignoring the advice of their biological and spiritual parents. Some even criticize these elderly guides, while choosing to do things their own way, as if they are beyond supervision. What such do not know is that not having or listening to spiritual parents can hinder progress in life.

It is to your great benefit therefore that you get close to elderly people who are spiritual, whose lifestyle is godly. They are the right kind of people to give you advice. They must have had a wide range of experiences on marital issues, which, together with the Spirit of God within them, put them in a better position to counsel you on what to do as you embark on the marital quest.

If your parents are not Christians - especially your mother - you need a lot of prayer and counseling. This becomes even more necessary if you suspect that your biological parents have a negative spirit. Your spiritual parents will have to help you more in this if you open your mind to them. They also could link you up with other ministers to add more fervency to their prayers.

It is generally believed that there is always an unending rift between a wife and her mother-in-law. There are many factors that could be responsible for such a rancorous relationship and it is usually more pronounced when the wife and her mother-in-law are under the same roof. It can sometimes be very difficult to resolve such mutual abhorrence, especially if it has spiritual undertones, with both women battling for supremacy over the other. This, notwithstanding, your prayer, as a Christian woman, is that God will help you to create an atmosphere of harmony in your home all the time.

3. See marriage as a serious matter.

Dear Sister, to be a wife is not a joke; it is a serious business and marriage can indeed be likened to a battlefield. Note that a wife is someone who becomes like a mother to her husband (see Genesis 24:67). Being with a husband therefore involves taking care of him till death do you part. This is why the marriage vow states that the commitment is "for better, for worse". It is too costly to enter into such a commitment without thinking of the implications.

Another reason marriage is a serious business is that

a wife indirectly becomes a servant of God through her husband. The Holy Spirit expresses this in Proverbs 31:11-12, "The heart of her husband safely trusts her; So he will have no lack of gain. She does him good and not evil All the days of her life."

You can imagine how easy it is for a man to die at the hand of his wife, since she is the one who cooks his food and takes care of some of his other fundamental needs. This is the reason I warn ladies to avoid pre-marital sex, and instead focus on getting to know their God-given husband, as it was in the case of Isaac and Rebekah (Genesis 24:44). If you allow yourself to be blinded by pre-marital sex or any other considerations and get married to the wrong man, you may end up becoming a murderer.

Bear in mind again that God has created and is specially preparing you to minister physically and spiritually to the need and existence of a particular man (1Corinthians 11:8-9). Therefore, it is not every man that can become "lord" to you as Sarah took Abraham; and it is not all men that can be said to be your husband, as the Lord pointed out to the Samaritan woman in John 4:16-19. Your preoccupation should thus be to have your own predestined husband once and for all. When you eventually find him, he will naturally prove to be caring, responsible and God-fearing. The true meaning of responsibility in marriage is "respond to my disability" – a trait that was evident in godly husbands like Abraham,

Isaac, Jacob, Noah and Joseph. They all responded appropriately to the disabilities of their wives.

YOU NEED A GODLY MAN

Truly, Jesus is our sustenance, but the man to whom you get married has his own part to play in your life – for good or for bad. This will depend on what choice you make and how you make it. I pray you will not marry a wrong man, in Jesus' name.

When seeking a man to marry, many ladies prefer to look for someone who is handsome and rich. Yet, God's word clearly states, "Favour is deceitful, and beauty is vain, but a woman [or man] that feareth the Lord, she [or he] shall be praised" (Proverbs 31:30). What these ladies do not realize is that since Satan knows that ladies tend to love flashy men, he sometimes makes his male agents to appear handsome and rich, order to blindfold the ladies under their influence. Through this, Satan has systematically linked many women with the wrong man. And as I have repeatedly mentioned, the effect upon their lives and destiny is often devastating, and many end up opting for divorce. This is the factor behind many of the problems in the world today.

Recent studies have revealed that in every hundred cases of crime, 90% of the perpetrators are from broken homes. The reason is because children from such homes easily fall prey to Satan's deceptions and manipulations.

DANGERS OF STRANGE MEN

In Proverbs 5:3-4, the Scripture speaks of the "strange woman", whose mouth is "smoother than oil" but whose end is as "bitter as wormwood." The same is true of getting married to a strange man – a man who is not your God-appointed husband. The result is always disastrous.

There was a godly woman who unknowingly married a strange man. In the course of their several years of marriage, they had six children together. However, after the birth of the sixth child, the man went out and befriended a strange woman who later became his second wife.

Out of the six children of the first wife, there was a lady who was particularly brilliant. She was diligent in her studies and soon became a medical doctor. One day, she wanted to celebrate her birthday with her fiancée. Sadly, while trying to prepare herself in her dressing room, a strange little breeze blew on her, and she fell down and became paralyzed. She was rushed to a hospital. But every effort made to restore her health proved abortive.

It reached a stage that she became incontinent and had to be wearing diapers. One day, the family concluded that she should be taken out to one spiritualist. On getting to the spiritualist, the man detected that the lady's predicament was his own handiwork. He confessed that it was her step-mother that had brought her case to him. He further explained that when the strange woman initially brought the case, he had told her that the lady could not be harmed but that she insisted he should tie her down. The spiritualist said he eventually complied by symbolically tying down a she-goat, and rendering it totally immobile.

Guess what? Immediately the man loosened the goat, the lady got up! Later on she was taken to London for proper care. After getting better, she settled in the city, practicing her profession and having a great time. Do you see the damage that a strange man can cause?

There is another case of a woman who got married to a carnal Christian. Shortly after they got married, the man lost his job, and since the wife believed that whatever she had belonged to her husband, she continued to give him a fixed sum of money every month. Unknown to her, he was always sharing the money with another woman – his mistress. When the wife eventually discovered what was going on, she confronted him about it. Shockingly, instead of the husband to apologize for wrongdoing, he began to batter his wife. It was a very pathetic case.

Then again there was a man who, in a bid to have a baby boy, purposely had eight children with his wife. Fortunately, the last child was a boy. Within the period of having these children, the family was in abject poverty. However, as soon as the condition of this man changed and he became wealthy, he considered his wife to be no more attractive and decided to have another woman.

One way or the other, the first wife was   poisoned and later died in the hospital. The man brought in the concubine that same year his first wife died. Can you imagine that?

Yet, these are just few of the numerous instances of the sorrows and heartaches inflicted on women by their strange husbands!

LEARN FROM ABRAHAM

You need to seriously sit down and take your Bible and read Abraham's way of getting a wife for his son in Genesis 24. You may be asking, "Why did he not get him a wife from the people he knew and the people from where he had been blessed? Why did he choose to go back to his country and to his people?"

The truth is that he wanted to avert future problem for Isaac, his only child. The Bible says "Remove not the ancient landmark, which thy fathers have set" (Proverbs 22:28). In other words, since Abraham has shown us a great example, we can safely follow his footsteps. He believed that it was God who guided him to marry Sarah, so he had to lead his son on the same route to search for his wife.

My dear sister, you are one of Abraham's daughters. Do not let anybody, including any so-called man or man of God, push you into a life mistake by telling you to marry someone who is not from the faith!

CHAPTER 4

MARRIAGE PRECAUTIONS AND PREPARATIONS

"Marriage is honourable in all, and the bed undefiled: but whoremongers and adulterers God will judge." (Hebrews 13:4)

Dear sister, let me begin this chapter by cautioning you not to ever allow any man to see your nakedness or have sex with you before marriage. You know why? God may want to use you as the Mary, Hannah, Elizabeth or the Shunammite woman of this generation. It is women like this that the Bible calls "great" women (2 Kings 4:8-10).

If you allow men to defile you, the purpose of God for your life may be diverted and your destiny may be destroyed - just because of a few minutes of pleasure. Satan always looks for loopholes in the lives of girls and women, in order to destroy them. Many women you see in town are not happy and well cared for. You know why? Because they married the wrong men and feel stuck because of their children. There are some who even try to change husbands but still end up in almost the same situation they left behind.

Why this cycle of disappointment and frustration? Because they started on a faulty foundation. The Bible says, "And even as they did not like to retain God in their knowledge, God gave them over to a reprobate mind, to do those things which are not convenient" (Romans 1:28). God allows the mistakes and regrets to continue until the individual acknowledges her fault and chooses to return to Him in repentance.

THE PLACE OF SEX

So, what exactly is the place of sex in a relationship? Sex is very important for marital peace, but it is not the end of love. Sex has a very powerful effect in your home with your husband; anything outside of this often comes with grave consequences. A lot of ladies fall into sexual deception and get impregnated before marriage. They believe that the man that is responsible for the pregnancy is their husbands. Well, God is gracious. Sometimes, it works out well but often it does not.

Sex outside marriage is not a demonstration of love but lust. Genuine love is caring, pure, kind, thinks no evil, rejoices not in iniquity, bears all things and is responsible. These positive traits are what should dominate your mind in entering into marriage, which will ultimately pave way for pure and enjoyable sex.

Sex must never be a deciding factor in choice of life-partner. The holy women who trusted in God believed and subjected themselves to their   husbands (1Peter 3:1-6). What they did was to focus on developing themselves in the nine components of the fruit of the Spirit (Galatians 5:22). This made it easier for them to recognize their God-ordained husbands and to regard such as their lords.

DANGER OF UNDUE INTIMACY WITH MEN

There are women who seem to enjoy being close to men, even more than their fellow women. They are often found in company of men whom they regard as simply "friends". Perhaps you are one of such. Note that you may be causing three major problems for yourself:

1. You may be hindering someone who has genuine interest in you from approaching you because the person may think you are already with someone else.

2. You may be exposing yourself to sexual harassment. A man's body system is different from a woman's, and anything could happen when least expected. This is how many ladies lose their virginity to unknown men because they are not aware of what is happening to them; they just find themselves in it, and from there they get unwanted pregnancies. Some even

commit abortion and die in the process. May the Lord help you, in Jesus' name.

3. You may be causing unwarranted suspicion and embarrassment to the entire church. The whole church may begin to think that you are engaged to someone or even indulging in sin with the person – not knowing that nothing of sort is really happening. The confusion will be from your carelessness.

I am further advising you not to keep company with ladies who go to their boyfriend's places, as the boyfriends may introduce their friends to you, which may lure you into sin.

What you need, sister, is more vigilant love. Don't be carried away by luxury and physical attractions which cannot last forever. You must be watchful against all end-time spirits that are dominating our society today. The Bible warns, "There is a way which seemeth right unto a man, but the end thereof are the ways of death" (See Proverbs14:12, 16:25, Genesis 31:33-35). To this end, you must strive to keep yourself holy for God, and He will in good time give you your own man.

Reasons to Avoid Casual Sex
- It is a satanic trap to destroy you.
- It kills your spiritual sensitivity and weakness your prayer life
- It causes backwardness in life.

- It causes terminal illness.
- It always brings the wrath of God upon the person.
- It makes you become powerless.
- It causes premature death.

Considerations in Marriage Preparation

The following are things to watch out for, when in courtship with a man:

- Physical maturity
- Financial buoyancy
- Spiritual maturity
- Moral strength
- Sincerity and constancy in love.

On your part, while planning to marry, you need to ask yourself, "Am I mature enough to marry, and am I financially ready? Do I have a spiritual anchor to sustain me in any marital problems? Does the man I want to marry really love me? Can I withstand the challenges of dealing with in-laws?

These are important things you should consider before going into marriage with any man because 95% of men go into marriage with ladies because of their beauty, education, family background or because of their posts in their jobs. This is why you must ensure the man really loves you, not because of anything else.

How can you get to know if a man really loves you? You may need to ask him these sixteen questions. The answers you receive will determine his readiness for a near future marriage. You need to do this prayerfully and not carelessly. Some men are present partners and not future partners. Some have inherited curses from their parents, which may hinder them from marrying and prospering. These are the reasons why these questions must be asked prayerfully and with all earnestness. You may be led to ask more or less. May the Holy Spirit lead and guide you in Jesus' name.

The questions are as follows:

- Why do you want to marry me?
- Do you really love me?
- What makes you to love me?
- Have you considered that my beauty may fade as I grow older?
- What are your future plans for me and our children?
- What do you know about me to warrant your choosing me?
- What does my level of education mean to you?
- I believe marriage is for better for worse. Have you considered some "worse" possibilities?
- Have you discussed your decision to marry me with your mother?

- Do your parents want you to marry now? Which tribe have they expressed their daughter-in-law to be from?

- How many ladies have you courted before?

- How many children have you had with other ladies?

- What is your belief about monogamy?

- Have you been jilted before? If yes, how many times and why?

- What is the present condition of those   ladies who jilted you?

- What do you think about the "one-purse" system in managing family's finances?

Again, please try to ask these questions step by step and take the answers to spirit-filled pastors or counselors to guide you on areas of confusion or concern.

The reason for the above questions is that some young men are not yet mature for marriage; but from a man's answers to these questions, you will know how ready and serious he is. Some young men's motive for being in love is for sexual gratification, and once this is settled, you become nothing to them. Some may be in love because of your beauty or the way you speak. It may be the way you walk, the way you dance or the way you sing. These are the things that normally intoxicate and drive some men into falling in love with a woman. You too must admit this as a reality, so as avoid positioning yourself for unserious interests. If you parade yourself before men with these personal qualities so that they may make advances towards you, then you will get what you want - present sexual partner and never a happy future partner.

NEED FOR DISCRETION

Please, note that, in asking the above questions, there is need to be careful, discreet and wise. It is not that a young man indicates his interest in you this evening and you begin to bombard him with these questions. No! You may ask him a few familiar ones like his full name, occupation and interests. You can also try to find out his readiness and maturity by letting him realize that you are prepared for a man who is prepared, and not just for a casual sex-partner. Then you tell him to give you some days to think and pray while asking him to do the same.

Actually, once you choose this approach, there is need for you to re-arrange your weekly schedule to include a day or days of fasting and prayer on marital wisdom and success. This man's name and other data will be major in that week's or month's prayer list. The next time you meet, you may let him know that you need to find out more details about him and his marital plans. Then pose some questions in a more serious but gentle manner. Emphasize prayer and fasting to him always and make sure there is no undue closeness. Let your discussion take place openly. There is no limit to how many times you keep on asking questions.

GETTING SUPPORT

You may not be able to get an answer to each of these questions by yourself. Especially as regards the spiritual condition of your suitor, you need your Pastor or other men of God that you can trust. In doing this, you need to be careful of so-called prophets or prophetesses. Still, God can lead you to a spirit filled one.

In actual fact, whatever answers you get from men of God are only meant to complement the ones the Holy Spirit has given you through dreams, the word of God, etc. Also, as earlier discussed, your parents-in-the-Lord are the most important people you can consult.

Another set of people you can consult are the leaders or workers of the church he claims to attend. You only ask about his seriousness at church secretly. You may not reveal that he talked to you.

Your parents' advice is also important, especially if they are also monogamous, or if they have a special interest in your marital life. You can know this if any of them has previously advised you biblically on marital issues.

RED FLAGS

There are responses to certain questions that should signal danger to you and make you to immediately reject a marriage proposal. These include:

1. Are you a Christian? "No".

2. Are you born-again "I am trying".

3. Do you have a girlfriend now? "Just one".

4. Which church do you attend? "No particular one".

5. Is your pastor aware of your marital plans? "No"

6. Can we go now to meet your Pastor? "Is that necessary?

7. Would you further need to seek God's face concerning this matter? "It is not necessary".

My advice to you about any man like this is, do not welcome him or consider him to be your future partner because the Bible says, we should not have anything to do with such a person(1 Corinthians 5:11).

CHAPTER 5

OBSTACLES TO A SUCCESSFUL MARRIAGE

"Take us the foxes, the little foxes, that spoil the vines: for our vines have tender grapes." (Song 2:15)

Now that you know the secrets of getting your own husband and the dangers of settling with a strange man, it is important to also be aware of the forces (or you can call them foxes) that often turn a marriage into a nightmare, so as to prevent them. Different marriage counselors have identified various obstacles to a successful marriage. Since experiences differ, I have itemized 17 of such obstacles here. I believe the Holy Spirit will reveal more to you as an individual. They are as follows:

1. Excessive temperamental similarity. This is when a husband and a wife have the same temperamental weaknesses, such that none is able to provide the needed contrast to ensure balance and stability in the home.

For instance, if each of the couple is quick-tempered or hot-tempered, the result will be constant conflict in the home.

2. Suspicions. Once there is lack of trust in the home, the juice of love, peace and harmony cannot flow as it should. This is why it is good to be mutually transparent, and also promptly address issues as they come.

3. Unforgiving spirit. Marriage has been rightly described as a union of two lifelong forgivers. No matter how rosy a relationship is, offences are bound to come and when steps are not quickly taken to discuss and forgive, crisis becomes inevitable.

4. Marital unfaithfulness. Unfaithfulness to the marital vows in any way opens the floodgate of distrust, frictions and even demonic manipulations.

5. Too much difference in family backgrounds. When the couple are from different social, cultural or racial backgrounds, it takes a lot of understanding, patience and maturity to prevent clashes in perspectives.

6. Weak spiritual appetite and strong desire for pleasure. Spiritual fervency is an indispensable lubricant for the wheels of progress and blessedness in a marriage. When any of the couple however prefers pleasure and luxury at the expense of spiritual matters, the marriage is bound to suffer.

7. Curses or spells upon any of the couple. This has

to do with the foundation. Any spiritual baggage from either of the couple that is not properly dealt with can constantly be a source of crisis for the household.

8. Determined sexual oppression. There is a reason the Bible specifically warns against this in 1 Corinthians 7:3-5. It is because it paves way for Satan to gain advantage over a family. This is why it must be avoided at all cost.

9. Impotency/infertility or any other disease. This can pose a serious challenge, especially when known and hidden before marriage. Otherwise, with true love, understanding and prayers, it can become a non-issue.

10. Third-party interferences, e.g. domestic helps, in-laws, relatives or friends. These are areas that must be properly discussed and addressed even before a marriage takes place. Thereafter, there must be caution, mutual agreement and spiritual discernment in handling these issues.

11. Diabolical attacks and manipulations. This can come from any angle. This is why a couple must be ever watchful and prayerful to keep the home fortified.

12. Disrespect to parents or church elders. No one likes to be disrespected or scorned. And this can get worse when directed at one's parents or other cherished people in one's life, such as spiritual leaders. Utmost discretion is required in all circumstances.

13. Too much gap in age difference and education.

This can create a problem due to clash of interests and mentalities.

14. Financial impropriety. When either of the couple is not transparent about family expenditures, or when there is mismanagement, flamboyance or partiality, things will definitely go wrong.

15. Transferred covenant on any of the couple. This is similar to unresolved curses. If any of the couple had entered into a covenant relationship with someone else before the marriage, it can open the door to unending crisis.

16. Immaturity in coping with marital stress. Marriage, as already noted, is a serious business and thus could sometimes involve some stress. If not properly handled with maturity and consideration, this could escalate to full-blown conflict.

17. Competition or leadership tussles in the home. This often arises from domineering tendencies and disregard for scriptural commands.

Dear sister, take note of your husband on these issues. If you realize that things are not going well, employ divine wisdom to get his attention to find out what could be wrong.

THE SNARE OF ADULTERY

Take note of the following tendencies that can lure a woman into adultery:

1. Love of money and covetousness.

2. Receiving gifts from members of the opposite sex.

3. Looseness and frivolousness with the opposite sex.

4. Welcoming ungodly discussions.

5. Idleness and worldliness.

6. Gluttony and excessive love of pleasure and luxury.

7. Inability to resist social functions and parties.

Sister, remember that nothing goes for nothing. Anytime you receive something from a man, it becomes more difficult for you to reject his demands. Most times, when you have collected a lot of things from a man, what he would require of you in return is your body for his sexual pleasure. This could lead to severe consequences, such as shame, regret, deadly diseases, unwanted pregnancy, broken relationship, demonic attacks and divine judgment. Therefore, Sister, abstain from the above pitfalls to safeguard your home and life.

TACKLING THE PROBLEM OF HOUSEMAID

It is no longer news that a lot of husbands indulge in sexual immorality with their housemaids. More often than not, this ultimately becomes a problem in their lives, as they soon begin to live a meaningless life because their destinies have been polluted by these girls. Whoever commits adultery with his housemaid will have his life turned upside because becoming a housemaid has some spiritual undertones. This is why you must be careful with whoever you employ as a housemaid.

A good wife, who really loves her husband, will not allow a housemaid to take over or be in control of the house. A wife who allows the housemaid to cook the best food for her husband, or assigns the housemaid to wash her husband's underclothes or dress his bed is to be pitied because she is gradually selling her home to her housemaid - and the housemaid may likely usurp it completely because the housemaid is not for your husband, but for you (Genesis 16:1, 30:3-9).

If you discover that your housemaid and your husband are getting too friendly, you must check the home system and be extra vigilant. If you discover anything negative, before asking your husband anything, send the stranger away and terminate her being with you. Do not let your husband know the day and time you will be taking that step because they can plan a meeting point and it will be like a coup against you.

It was the above mistakes that Sarah made and it caused her a lot of problems. It was not until Hagar was sent out of her home that she was able to have rest of mind (Genesis 21:10-13). Remember that God told Abraham that his wife, Sarah, would bear him a son. But because of her temporary barrenness, Sarah made her maid, Hagar, to become too intimate with her husband and he ended up impregnating her (Genesis 16). However, God did not recognize Hagar as a wife; He only knew Sarah. It was that mistake that gave birth to Ishmael, and Ishmael's generation gave birth to the Islamic world; and you already know what Islam means to Christendom.

I urge you therefore, sister, do not sell your home to any strange girl or woman. They can be very crafty and cunning, and can systematically destroy your home. If your housemaid is painting her nails or using make-up in your home, ask yourself a question: who is she doing it to attract or impress? You or your husband? It is a dangerous thing. Do not allow it in your house.

Housemaids have sent some women out of their homes by having sexual relationship with their husbands and polluting the children with stealing, drunkenness and fornicating spirit. And if care is not taken, the housemaid will give birth for the husband and the real wife will become a fugitive in her own home.

Many homes become polluted by so called housemaids because the real women of the house are lazy. When the housemaid is allowed to take over the maintenance of the home, it becomes a problem. In some homes with houseboys, it is the houseboy who deflowers the daughters of the house because of the carelessness of the parents. In some places, it is the housemaid who trains the sons how to have sex. All these satanic attitudes may cause you everlasting destruction. So, sister, beware!

CHAPTER 6

DEALING WITH THE PROBLEM OF FOREIGN CULTURE

It may not sound reasonable to you, but it has been confirmed several times that several sincere ladies have missed their God-given husbands because of avoidable mistakes, arising from culture conflict. You have to know that as you approach the age of marriage, one of the things men begin to watch is how you are able to bridle your appetite for foreign behaviors and tendencies. Even westerners themselves admire the African culture because it celebrates virtue and soberness.

Several parents have threatened to disown their sons if they continue dating women who are loose in dressing! Where a young man insists on going ahead with his decision, things are usually made tough for the in-coming lady.

It is the same crisis that sometimes befalls ladies whom God has given the opportunity of enviable professions or academic pursuits that have exposed them to foreign cultures. Some of these women allow their exposures to make them act indiscreetly, with attitudes and behaviors that seem to disparage their local culture or that of their in-laws. You have to be aware that certain gestures and attitudes are considered rude or unacceptable, depending on the culture of the people you are relating with.

Let's assume you are on a visit to your in-laws or prospective in-laws and you sit down on a spot, while dishing out instructions to the boys and girls in the home - as you would do in your office or shop. This will certainly infuriate the elders in the home as they will take your behavior as a reflection of arrogance and may develop a dislike for you.

Although you may have a different motive for some of the things you do, if you do not apply wisdom and discretion, they may be misinterpreted. For instance, you may be the type that loves to dress to express yourself, without bothering about what people would say. If you do not exercise caution in dressing around your in-laws, they may consider you to be a loose or uncultured woman and from that moment develop a wrong impression of you. Even when they have not assessed you spiritually, you would have made them to practically write you off because of your inability to demonstrate discretion.

More specifically, you must be especially careful when you visit your parents-in-law. Please, respect them in the way they understand respect. If it requires kneeling down to greet them, please do that; or if it needs using your two hands to give them something, while curtsying, please do that. That is what we call culture and tradition in Africa, especially in Nigeria. Be aware that everybody in your husband's family is watching your movement and behavior, to know the kind of wife you are or will turn out to be.

HUMILITY PAYS

You may argue that as an astute lawyer, newscaster, or someone who is naturally outspoken, should you suddenly become an introvert because you are with your in-laws? Or as a medical doctor or scientist, you may wonder, "Do I just look on like a moron when I know things are not the way they ought to be? Or, "As an accountant that is wise and versatile in many things, do I give in to foolish decisions because of my in-laws who may not see things in the same perspective with me?" The answer to all these is YES, as it will save you from unnecessary hassles. The Bible emphasizes the place of wisdom in all our dealings thus, "If the iron be blunt, and he do not whet the edge, then must he put to more strength: but wisdom is profitable to direct" (Ecclesiastes 10:10).

Never allow the exposure from your profession or education to constitute a barrier to your marital success. If you humble yourself to speak the local dialect of your in-laws or in-laws to be, you are not being hypocritical or condescending; you are only paving way to gain more friendship with your in-laws. Try this and see how your in-laws will fall in love with you. But if you insist on "being yourself" and flaunting your knowledge and high status, you will end up creating unnecessary rifts and suspicions. Your in-laws may think you are a potential trouble-maker, while you may think that his parents don't really want him to marry you. Yet, none of this is true. So, try to make necessary adjustments in everything you do.

WATCH YOUR FRIENDSHIP

You must learn to be careful with so-called friends. To start with, it is not always wise to start discussing the person you want to marry with anybody, for the purpose of gossiping, bragging or sharing testimonies. Except the friend is one of your spiritual mentors that can guide you in God's way, trust no one. Somebody you call a friend may be an enemy spiritually. If she knows that this is a person that God sent to you and he is your messiah, she may from that moment arrange spiritual attack against your marriage, and if care is not taken, you may not succeed due to your ignorance and carelessness.

Many women's husbands have been hijacked by so called friends and cousins. Some have lost their husbands to witchcraft attacks, leading to incessant quarrels, accidents, loss of jobs etc. The supposed close friends of some women have systematically taken their husbands and sent them out of their homes. This happened because they were busy telling their friends the positive stories of their husbands or by allowing the close enemies they called friends to be frequent in their homes to see how well they were, not knowing that they were stoking the fire of jealousy and enmity.

DEFENDING YOUR HUSBAND

If your husband cannot perform well sexually or maybe he recently developed a problem that makes him to perform less than normal, it is unwise to start up a quarrel or make jest of him. What the situation requires is great care and understanding from you.

Again, this is not the time to bruise his ego by spurning his demand for sexual intimacy. There is no need to flare up or to tease and taunt your husband, whether in word or in action. What a virtuous woman would do is to start praying secretly and allowing him to have as much intimacy as he wants. It is then the Holy Spirit will eventually work through you to heal him.

You should also be aware that the problem with your husband could be an arrow targeted at frustrating you. And if you choose to handle it carnally, for instance, divorcing him, you may still find the same problem occurring in your new marriage. Moreover, your husband could go and marry another woman and eventually have a settled home, to your shame.

Satan is always interested in destroying marriages. He knows that homes belong to God, including your husband. His intention could be to send you out of your matrimonial home and back to your father's house, whereas your father's home is a temporary place for you and not your permanent home. The Bible says, "Hearken, O daughter, and consider, and incline thine ear; forget also thine own people, and thy father's house; So shall the king greatly desire thy beauty: for he is thy Lord; and worship thou him" (Psalm 45:10-11).

Do you understand what the Bible is saying here? It simply means, listen, sister, forget your father (your biological parents) including everything there. It is only then your husband will love you, because he is your visible lord. Satan knows this fact and that is the reason he always wants to destroy homes.

To this end, try to understand your husband in everything he does. You need to take care of him as your first son. Physically and spiritually, he is your father; you are to make him happy all the time and by this, he will be able to make some good decisions about your well-being and the betterment of the family. Forget about who you are in your office and who you are in your father's house and show your husband good love and respect.

DON'T TAKE OVER

Here is another essential advice that requires your utmost

attention. Your husband has been ordained by God to be the captain of the ship of your life (Genesis 3:16). Moreover, God categorically says in Ephesians 5 that you must submit to your husband as unto the Lord Himself (Ephesians 5:22). To this end, it is not expected of you to be speaking authoritatively to your husband or playing the role of the leader in the home or trying to dominate the home. This always leads to trouble.

As a good wife, you should always try to look for a convenient time to talk to your husband in such a way that he will listen. He may already be battling with some issues at his place of work and expects to be able to rest at home. It would be wrong for you to add to his burden by upsetting him again.

There was the case of a woman who had five children for her husband. Sadly, at a point, the woman felt so secure in her marriage that she was no longer vigilant about house chores and necessary marital responsibilities. She even neglected praying and studying the Bible and became very stubborn with her husband. It was at this point her husband pulled out and got involved with a strange woman. Soon after, he brought the woman home. The strange woman also had five children. Could you believe that the all the five children of the first woman ran mad? Enquiries were made spiritually in many places; it was the hand of the strange woman they always identified. The problem got to the point that the first son wanted to have sex with his own mother! This made the first wife to leave the home. The strange woman was still in that home up till the time of this writing. You see how Satan systematically destroyed a good home? No wonder the Bible says, "The thief cometh not, but for to steal, and to kill, and to destroy…" (John 10:10)

In case you are passing through a similar condition as described above, my counsel is that you should submit yourself to God. Let 60% of any prayer you offer to God be about your husband and 20% for your children and the remaining 20% for yourself and your parents. Proverbs 14:1 says, "Every wise woman buildeth her house: but the foolish plucketh it down with her hands." Sister, remember, if you keep silent over your husband's problems, it means you are planning to destroy your future indirectly and systematically.

Let me quickly cite another example here. A lady was planning to wed, and when it remained two weeks, the lady came to my friend for prayer. It was from there a prophecy came out that she should not take any garment from anybody to wear, otherwise she would lose her life.

Later, this lady travelled to her hometown to verify the arrangements for the wedding from her father. Unexpectedly, her father's younger sister bought a complete native attire, known in Yorubaland as aso oke and insisted that she must wear it. Her father's younger sister turned it to a quarrel and started insulting the lady. Her mother who did not know what was going on asked the lady to wear the attire, but the lady called her mother to a private room and told her the prophetic word from God. After the discussion, the mother asked her sister-in-law to leave the dress and that the young woman would wear it later. To everyone's surprise, the woman refused and insisted that the lady must wear it before she went away. It was at this point that the lady's mother confronted the woman and asked her if she had any ulterior motive for her insistence. Unable to answer, the woman went away.

What the family of the lady did afterwards was to cancel the wedding arrangements and subsequently arranged for a private wedding, devoid of any extravagance and known to only a few family members of the bride and the groom.

FURTHER PRECAUTIONS

Please do not rush into marriage, so as not to rush out of it. Do not marry an archenemy or somebody that will sink your glory, in the name of having a husband or getting married. Take note that if a million men admire your beauty, not all of them will marry you or be your husband. Nobody loves you, except the man that takes you to the altar.

To this end, I must repeat that you should not let anybody take you to bed and mess you up sexually because, once you are deflowered, you can never regain it again. And if your real husband is somebody that cherishes virginity and if it is not there by the time he marries you, it is capable of destroying the love and confidence he has in you. He may not even tell you the reason for changing his attitude towards you.

Remember, your primary assignment in your marital life is to take care of your husband. He should be the first thing in your life and nothing should disturb you in doing this - not your parents, business, or even your children. Whatever he may have wrongly done to you, discuss with him and forgive and forget. Continue to serve him. This is what makes a home to be happy and stand strongly. Remember, the Bible says, "Lest Satan should get an advantage of us: for we are not ignorant of his devices" (2 Corinthians 2:11). Satan always schemes, but I pray he does not get you in Jesus' name.

Finally, if the person proposing to marry you demands for sex before the day of your marriage, be 100% sure that he has a hidden agenda and he's looking for somebody he will take to hell.

CHAPTER 7

NECESSITY OF MATURITY

"...strong meat belongeth to them that are of full age, even those who by reason of use have their senses exercised to discern both good and evil." (Hebrews 5:14)

Maturity is the state of being able to independently reason, act and manage problems. Maturity often comes with age, but age is not always a determinant of maturity. Marriage can sometimes be stressful, but a mature person will always find a way to manage it, without allowing it to cause further problems. The immature person, on the other hand, gets easily stressed about the most trivial issues that should normally be overlooked. And before you know it, the person is already fed up of marriage and thinking of divorce.

So, the question is, are you mature enough to cope with the demands of marriage? In answering this question, you have to consider the four areas of maturity, which are the physical, the emotional, the mental, and the spiritual before determining your readiness for marriage.

PHYSICAL MATURITY

Yes, you may consider yourself physically mature, but the truth is that physical maturity doesn't come at the same time for every female. Some young women feel mature enough for marriage at 18 years of age, while others feel they are not ready yet, even at 28 years! In truth, age of maturity cannot be generally fixed; however, I would advise that you ensure that you are not younger than 20 years in order to allow your reproductive organs to be as ready as possible.

Another area of physical maturity is your size. There are special cases in which a female looks far bigger or smaller than one would expect of someone of her age. Men easily get carried away by female bodies that look robust and fully mature, and if you are not careful, at 16 years, you may get deceived by all the attention you get and start thinking of marriage. But as we have already observed, readiness for marriage goes beyond physical maturity.

On the other hand, if you do not see men coming to you because of your small stature at 25 years of age, you need not feel ashamed or dejected. Take your case to God. He will send you your suitable husband and make your life a testimony. There is definitely solution for you in Jesus Christ. He is the way out of pain into pleasure. He is the way out of mourning into melody. He is the way out of gloom into glory. He is the way out of troubles into testimonies. He is the way out of regret into rejoicing. You only need to intensify your prayers and social interactions.

EMOTIONAL MATURITY

This involves your ability to bear stress, resulting from pain, hurt, misunderstanding, loss or change in circumstances. If little matters often get you crying and feeling frustrated, you are not emotionally mature. Moreover, you must also be able to manage positive emotions, such as joy or feeling of accomplishment and satisfaction. Life is sometimes unpredictable. Thus, if care is not taken, joy may soon turn to sadness and accomplishment may give way to depression.

The home training you obtained from your parents or guardian is very essential to your success in marriage, especially if you did enjoy a healthy family environment. Many ladies believe that once they leave the tertiary institution, they are mature for marriage. They forget that academic knowledge is of little or no use in handling marital issues. What helps most times is a combination of divine wisdom and lessons from parents/guardians and the church. This is why you need the church's Sunday school, conferences, growth committee or counseling group to guide you from time to time.

The experiences of other married couples are also very essential. These will prepare your mind towards what to expect from your man. Christian books on courtship, marriage and home-keeping like this one in your hand are necessary. Attending marriage seminars and discussions are compulsory, at least, two years before you start to plan for this great experience of your life.

SPIRITUAL MATURITY

Your personal study and understanding of the Bible is extremely important because without spiritual knowledge, mental knowledge is useless. Systematic study of the Bible must have been part and parcel of your life, at least, three to five years before you start planning for marriage. As you require personal study of the Bible, so also do you need prayer, fasting and personal practice of holiness.

Spiritual maturity is very important because you never can tell the exact spiritual level of the man you want to marry. If he is a pastor or someone who believes in the efficacy of the prayer of a believer, he may ask you to lead a prayer session with some people, or to go to some people in the church and pray for them if they are sick or having problems. On the other hand, he may be someone who has knowledge but not deep understanding of Scripture. It may happen that for some very crucial reason, you are not able to give in to his sexual demands for a night. He may want to insist by citing 1 Corinthians 7:2, "Nevertheless, to avoid fornication, let every man have his own wife, and let every woman have her own husband." Such a man may need to be reminded that the same Bible says in 1 Corinthians 7:5, "Defraud ye not one the other, except it be with consent for a time, that ye may give yourselves to fasting and prayer…" How will you be able to help such a man or even your children without being spiritually sound and having adequate understanding of the scriptures?

In addition to all that has been said so far, let me say that going for counseling could help you. Deliverance clinic could be necessary for both of you. Going for medical tests – to know genotype, HIV status etc – is important. Moreover, to assert that God is the one leading you is not enough; you also need to know your health compatibility. It is equally dangerous for you to base your decision to go into marriage with someone on the content of your dream. There have been cases where hypnotic influence is used to make a lady to see herself married to someone that she would never have ordinarily considered. Exercise utmost caution. Prophecies sometimes come from the minds of some supposed prophets rather than from the Spirit of God. If a man of God entices you into marriage, he will rule your home.

KEEP YOURSELF PURE

Dear sister, do you know that it was the way Ruth kept herself that made Boaz to marry her? She distinguished herself among other ladies in the society. Although Ruth was not a virgin, she dedicated herself totally to God;

and by that, she became a spiritual virgin (Ruth 3:10). Are you keeping your body for God and Christ or for human beings?

There was a lady that fell in love with an Indian who had been giving her money and many things. One day, he took her to a hotel and asked her for sex and she succumbed. What the man had with her was what they call "oral sex". The third day, she started feeling that something was moving in her womb. This continued until she went for deliverance. Before then, she had been taken to a hospital and the X-ray had detected that a snake was moving in her womb!

Let me give you another example. There was a sister who ignored the will of God in marriage and got married to a wrong man who was a prominent person in society. What happened was that God had told a young man to go and approach her for marriage but she had refused the proposal because the young man was not rich. God sent somebody to warn her that the brother was her husband but she refused. Her mind was bent on her plan to marry the rich, influential and well-connected man. When she eventually got married to the wealthy man, there was no fruit of the womb for several years. This made them to search for the reason. It was later that a prophet told them that their problem was from the woman. She had left the person she ought to marry and had rejected the will of God. It was later that God told her to go and meet the man and apologize for what she had done. After that, she got pregnant in the eighth year of marriage.

BEAUTY OF SUBMISSION

A good way of demonstrating all-round maturity is your ability to submit to your husband, as the Bible says in Ephesians 5:22-24, "Wives, submit yourselves unto your own husbands, as unto the Lord. For the husband is the head of the wife, even as Christ is the head of the church: and he is the saviour of the body. Therefore as the church is subject unto Christ, so let the wives be to their own husbands in every thing."

Love and submission make the home to be a heaven on earth. So, sister, seek to submit yourself to your husband in everything – except in matters that contradict God's word. This is what makes a home to be stable and peaceful. When you turn your husband to a housemaid or you look down on him, things cannot go well in that house. This is also why you must have your God-ordained husband – so that submission will be easy and so that you can have rest of mind.

The case of the woman at the well in John 4 bears witness to this. She had no rest of mind and was moving from man to man because she was yet to find her God-ordained husband. Even Jesus confirmed it when He told her, "Thou hast well said, I have no husband: For thou hast had five husbands; and he whom thou now hast is not thy husband: in that saidst thou truly" (17-18).

Even if a woman becomes a professor or a billionaire, without having her real husband, she will not have rest of mind. This reminds me of a one-time chairperson and managing director of a bank. She seemed to have everything in the world, but lack of submission ended her first marriage. Then she remarried but things remained the same. She ended up living alone and unfulfilled.

I urge you, sister, strive to submit to your husband, so that peace will reign in your life and home in Jesus' name.

CHAPTER 8

YOUR PRIMARY ASSIGNMENT

"That they may teach the young women to be sober, to love their husbands, to love their children, To be discreet, chaste, keepers at home, good, obedient to their own husbands, that the word of God be not blasphemed." (Titus 2:4-5)

Many married women have lost sight of their primary and original assignment. They no longer focus upon the assignment given to them by God. Many seek professional recognition, political greatness or even church leadership while leaving their home responsibilities to domestic helps. Many times, these domestic helps exploit their mistresses' careless attitude to wreak havoc in the home and exert negative influence on the children. The children eventually grow to become miscreants in the society.

Let me emphasize it here. A married woman's primary assignment is caring for her home. It is what women achieve in the home that molds the society and the whole world. Sadly, Satan has blindfolded many to this great assignment from God. They forget that if a woman cannot properly manage a home, then the world cannot be a settled place.

Recall that it was Sarah's hospitality that produced Isaac. She promptly joined her husband to entertain angels without knowing it, and this brought her the fruit of the womb. It was Hannah's godliness and prevailing prayers that produced Samuel. It was the way Elizabeth held her house that produced John the Baptist. And it was Mary's virtuousness that qualified her to be the vessel through which our Lord Jesus Christ came to the world.

SEARCH FOR WISE WOMEN

The Bible says, "Every wise woman buildeth her house: but the foolish plucketh it down with her hands" (Proverbs 14:1). So, where are the wise women in our society today? I mean women like Ruth Elton, Aimee Semple McPherson, Kathryn Kuhlman and Maria Woodworth Etter? They have all gone out in search of public offices and political posts. They all want to accumulate wealth and worldly acclaim.

Don't get me wrong here. There's nothing bad in a woman seeking public office, doing business or making money. But the home comes first. The people you want to lead in the public were raised by a woman in a home. And the moral decay in our society that we often complain about came because women have neglected their roles.

To this end, I am using this medium to appeal to our mothers and married women in general to go back home and perform the original assignment given to them by God, before it is too late. It is then that our nation will have a future and there will be hope for our children.

WIFELY ROLES

Please, take note that the wife has several roles at home. First and foremost of these is being a mother, exhibiting the natural motherly care to her husband and children. As a mother who protects her children from all forms of attacks, her concern for her home should have no limit.

The wife never harbors malice or vengeful spirit towards her husband. She is full of the milk of love and mercy and ever ready to forgive and forebear any wrong done against her by her husband. She deliberately tunes up the positive side of her husband's nature and attitude. She loves him unconditionally.

A good wife does not seek her own selfish ends. She does not quarrel with her in-laws. She always loves to entertain visitors and keeps the house tidy. She does not backbite with ungodly women around the streets or associate with them. She appreciates her husband as the best gift from God to her and is ever grateful to God for this and always prays for him.

TIMELY REMINDER

As I wrap up this book, I need to re-emphasize a few points, as a way of summary. The issue of waiting upon the Lord in the area of marriage cannot be over-emphasized. Some marriages are concluded based on many wrong factors. A good Christian woman should not just jump at any man; nor allow any man to have carnal knowledge of her before marriage, as this could lead to a lifetime of destruction and regret.

Embrace chastity, both in the secret and in the open, and you can be sure that you'll certainly have more than enough reward and blessing to enjoy from God. As a child of God, yield your totality to Him as a holy and living sacrifice.

God has infinite wisdom to give you His best. He is awesome, powerful and wonderful. Don't settle for His permissive will, instead of His perfect one. Do not put the Lord God to the test (Luke 4:12). Wait on Him for your appointed time. Those who wait upon Him are never put to shame.

If you have decided to get married, I rejoice with you. But ensure to consider and meditate on all we have discussed so far. It will do you a lot of good if you study them one after the other as a checklist before you commit yourself to anyone. The Holy Spirit will use the message to guide you as you go about with your plans.

CHAPTER 9

PRAYER POINTS FOR A BLISSFUL HOME

"Be anxious for nothing, but in everything by prayer and supplication, with thanksgiving, let your requests be made known to God." (Philippians 4:6, NKJV)

Prayer is the master key to open all that you, as a child of God, need to open and to shut out those things that are contrary to God's wonderful purpose for every area of your life, including marriage. From the moment you begin to consider marriage, you must make prayer for a godly, blessed and happy home a frequent engagement.

I have compiled a list of prayer points here to serve as a guide for you. However, for your prayer to be meaningful, acceptable and effective, you need to take the following crucial steps:

1. Confess your sins to God in true repentance and ask

for His forgiveness and cleansing. "If we confess our sins, He is faithful and just to forgive us our sins and to cleanse us from all unrighteousness." (1 John 1:9).

"I tell you, Nay; but, except ye repent ye shall all likewise perish." (Lk 13:3). "Repent ye therefore, and be converted, that your sins may be blotted out" (Act 3:19).

2. Forsake every sin you have confessed of, as well as every doubt, fear and worry.

"Let the wicked forsake his way, and the unrighteous man his thoughts; let him return to the Lord, and He will have mercy on him; and to our God, for He will abundantly pardon" (Isaiah 55:7).

3. Believe you are forgiven and made a child of God, and that God will guide you into a blissful marriage.

"For with the heart man believeth unto righteousness; and with the mouth confession is made unto salvation. For the scripture saith, Whosoever believeth on him shall not be ashamed" (Romans 10:10-11).

4. Resolve to wholeheartedly walk in God's way and not be moved by the dictates of the world.

"Thus says the Lord: "Stand in the ways and see, and ask for the old paths, where the good way is, and walk in it; then you will find rest…"(Jeremiah 6:16).

PRAYER POINTS

1. O Lord, let every manipulation of Satan over my life, foundation and marriage scatter, in Jesus' name.

2. O God, you are the giver of life, give me my own husband by your own divine arrangement, in Jesus' name.

3. O Lord, perfect my marriage in all areas, in Jesus' name.

4. O Lord, prove your ownership of my life in every area, in Jesus' name.

5. O Lord, destroy every satanic plan fashioned against my marital life, in Jesus' name.

6. O Lord, let your will consume my will in my marriage, in Jesus' name.

7. Holy Spirit, blow upon me such that, sin will have no more place in my life, in Jesus' name.

8. O Lord, send the axe of fire and destroy every evil deposit in my foundation, in Jesus' name.

9. O Lord, refine and purge my heart by the blood of Jesus, in Jesus' name.

10. O Lord, collect for me all my divine goodness that my husband has trampled upon, in Jesus' name.

11. Wherever men have wounded me, heal me O Lord, in Jesus' name.

12. Any evil mark that men have placed on my body, be wiped off by the blood of Jesus, in Jesus' name.

13. Every area that men are tormenting me, Lord, deliver and comfort me, in Jesus' name.

14. Lord, come into my life and renew my life, in Jesus' name.

15. Lord, according to your word, contend with every power or personality waging war against my marriage and destiny, in Jesus' name.

16. Almighty God, let my divinely-appointed husband come forth and locate me, in Jesus' name.

17. Dear Father, let the showers of your blessings rain down upon my marital life, in Jesus' name.

18. Spirit of God, fill me with abundant grace and exceeding wisdom to be the ideal wife of an ideal husband, in Jesus' name.

19. Lord, shield my life and home from every negative and demonic influence, in Jesus' name.

20. Father, I thank you because I know my prayers are answered and that you will do far above my requests.

"Now unto him that is able to do exceeding abundantly above all that we ask or think, according to the power that worketh in us, Unto him be glory in the church by Christ Jesus throughout all ages, world without end. Amen." (Ephesians 3:20-21)

Kindly tell others about this book and spread its message far and wide.

If you have any marital problem, please don't hesitate to contact us for counseling. Or, if you need our ministry for seminars, conferences, Bible lectures or symposiums in your church or fellowship, please write, visit or call for further help. Keep growing, keep moving and keep watching. Remember, Jesus is the Lord!

Thank you and God bless you.